HammerHead
SHARK
COLORING BOOK
FOR KIDS

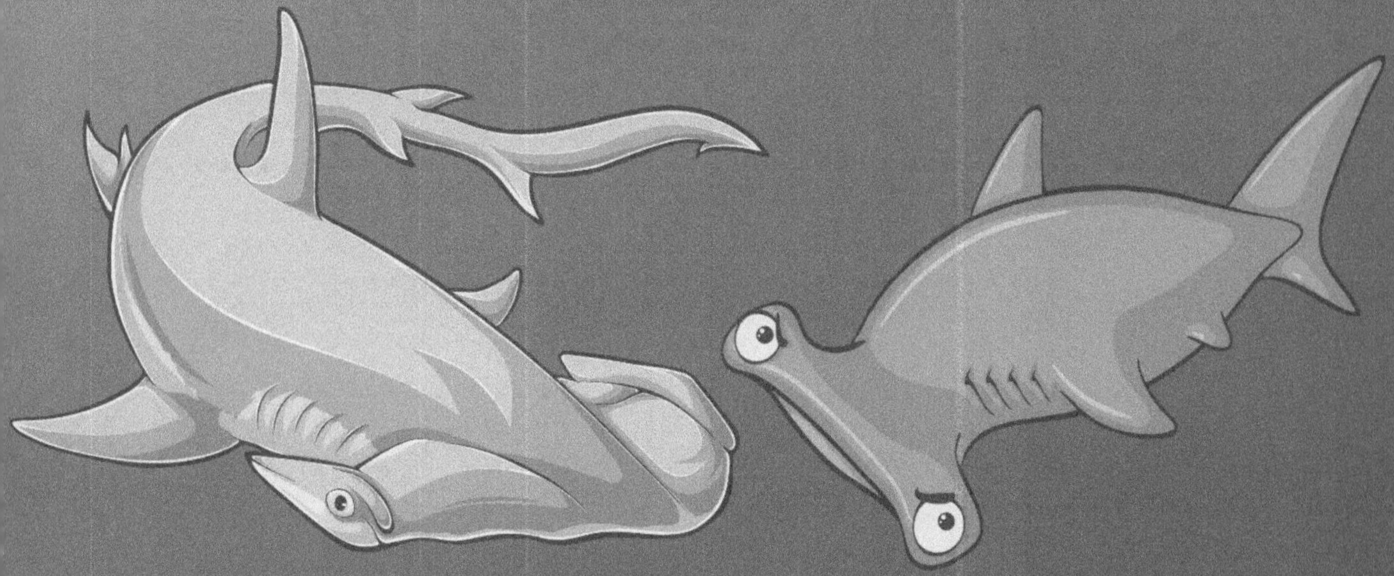

allrounder Press House

THIS BOOK BELONGS TO:

EXPERIENCE THE SIMPLE JOY OF SHARK COLORING BOOK

- HOURS OF ENTERTAINING BRAIN EXERCISE
- STRESS-RELIEVING COLORING PRACTICE
- A VARIETY OF INTERESTING COLORING THEMES
- EASY TO TEAR OUT, THANKS TO WIDE MARGINS

For More Word Search Puzzle, Maze Puzzle, Sudoku, Alphabet Tracing and also Coloring Book Please Visit Our Author Page

HAPPY COLORING

allrounder Press House

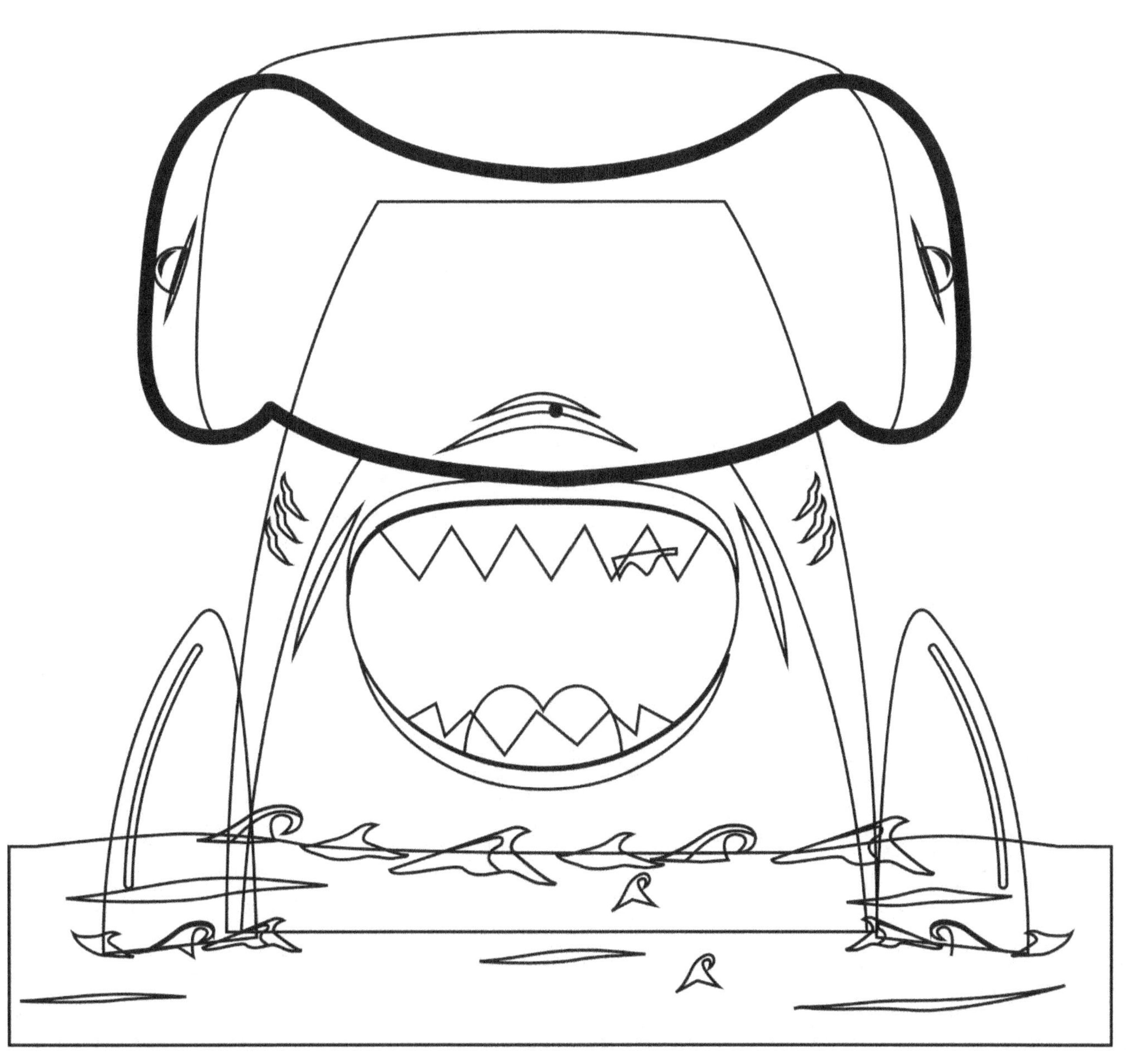

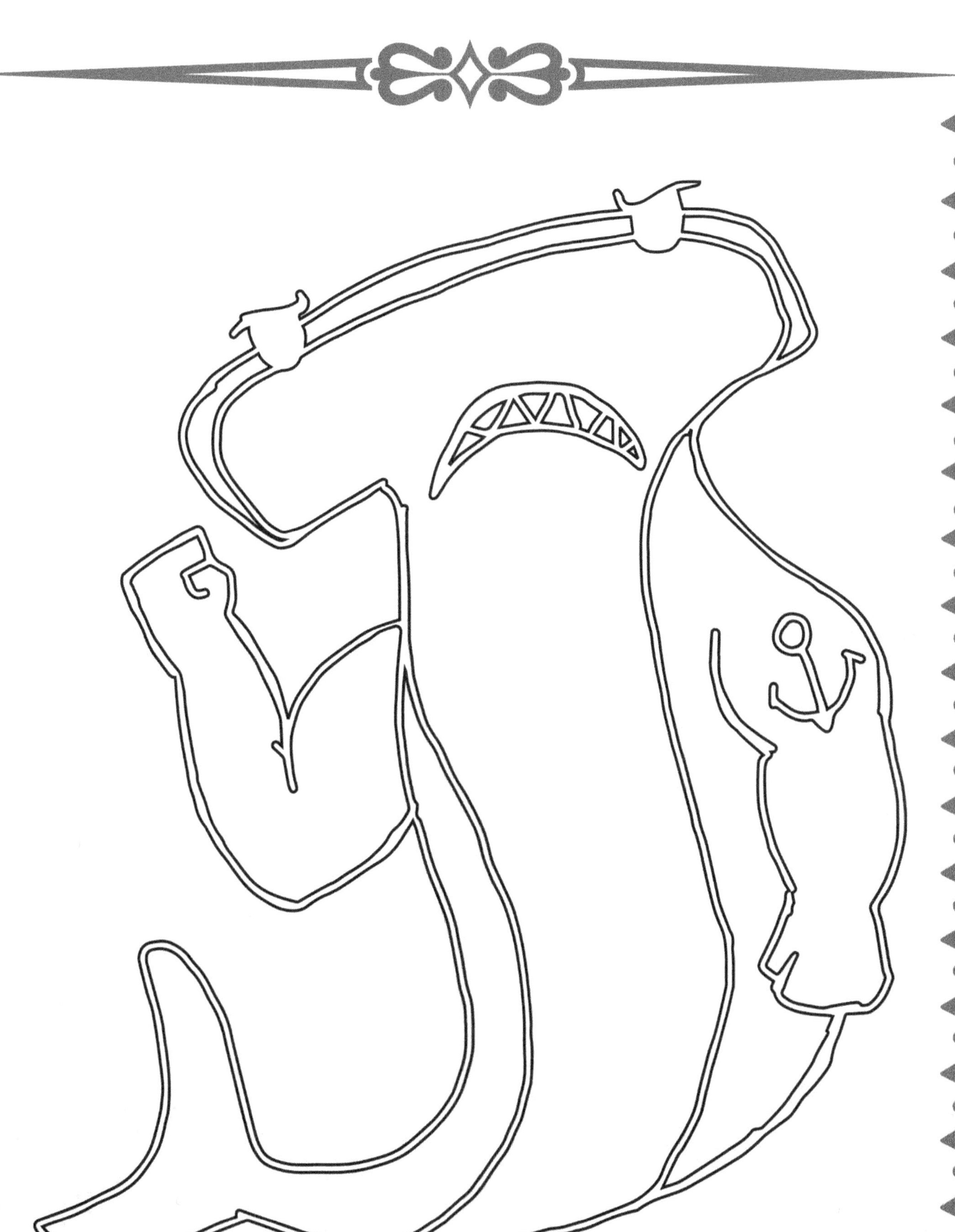

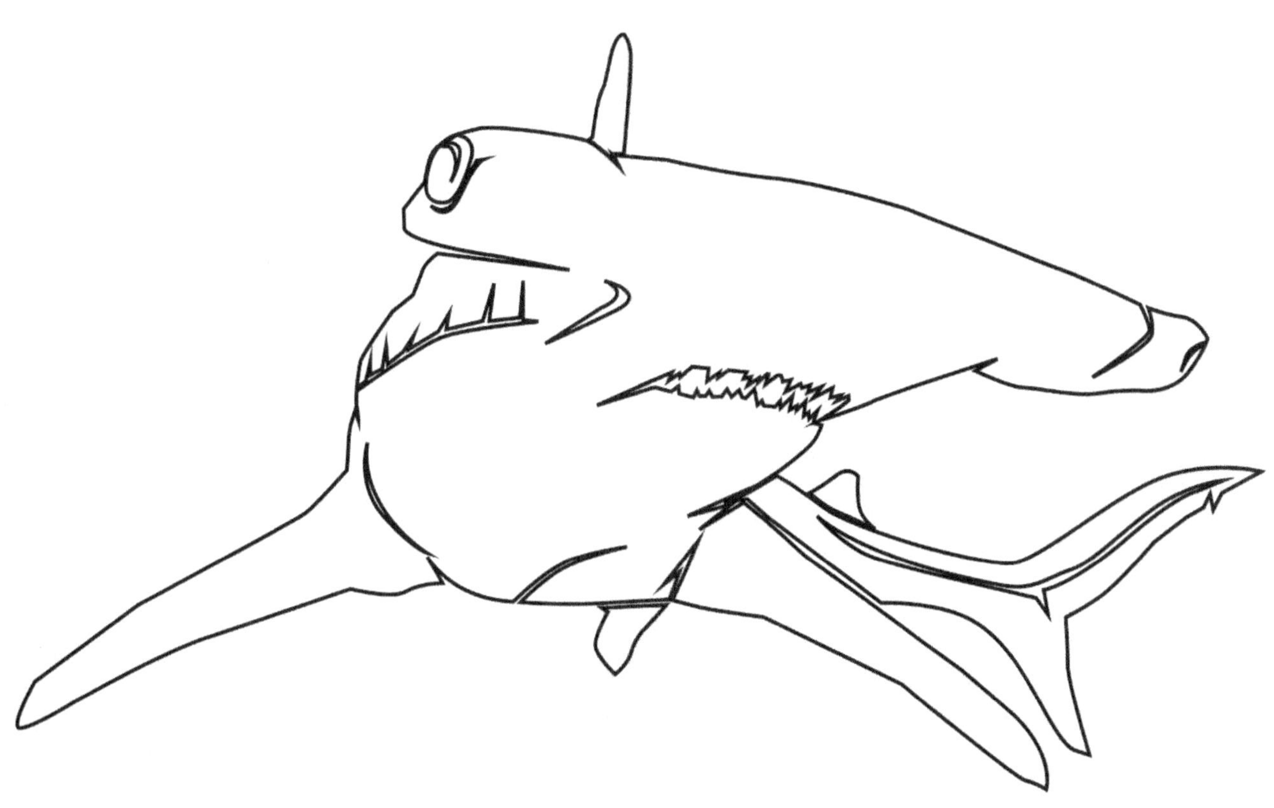

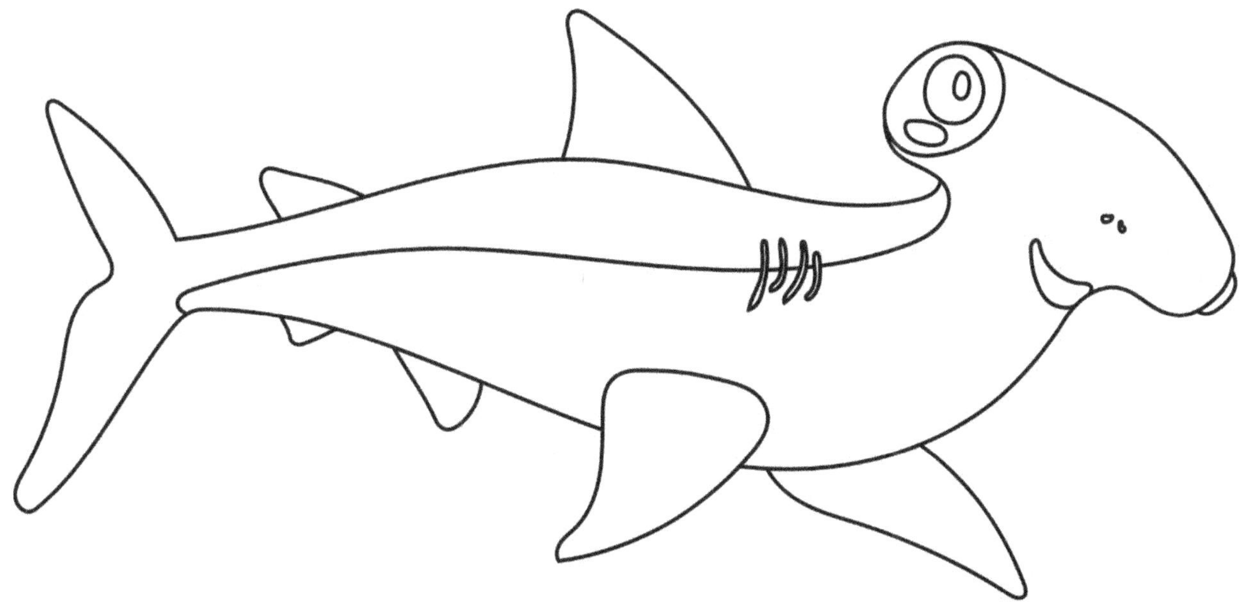

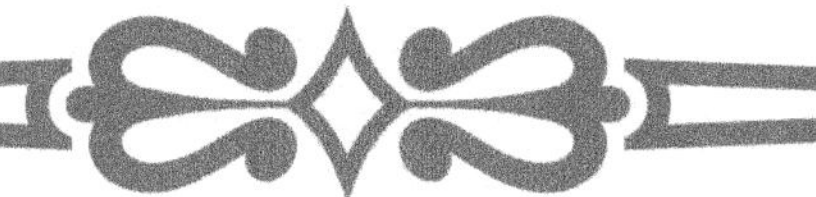

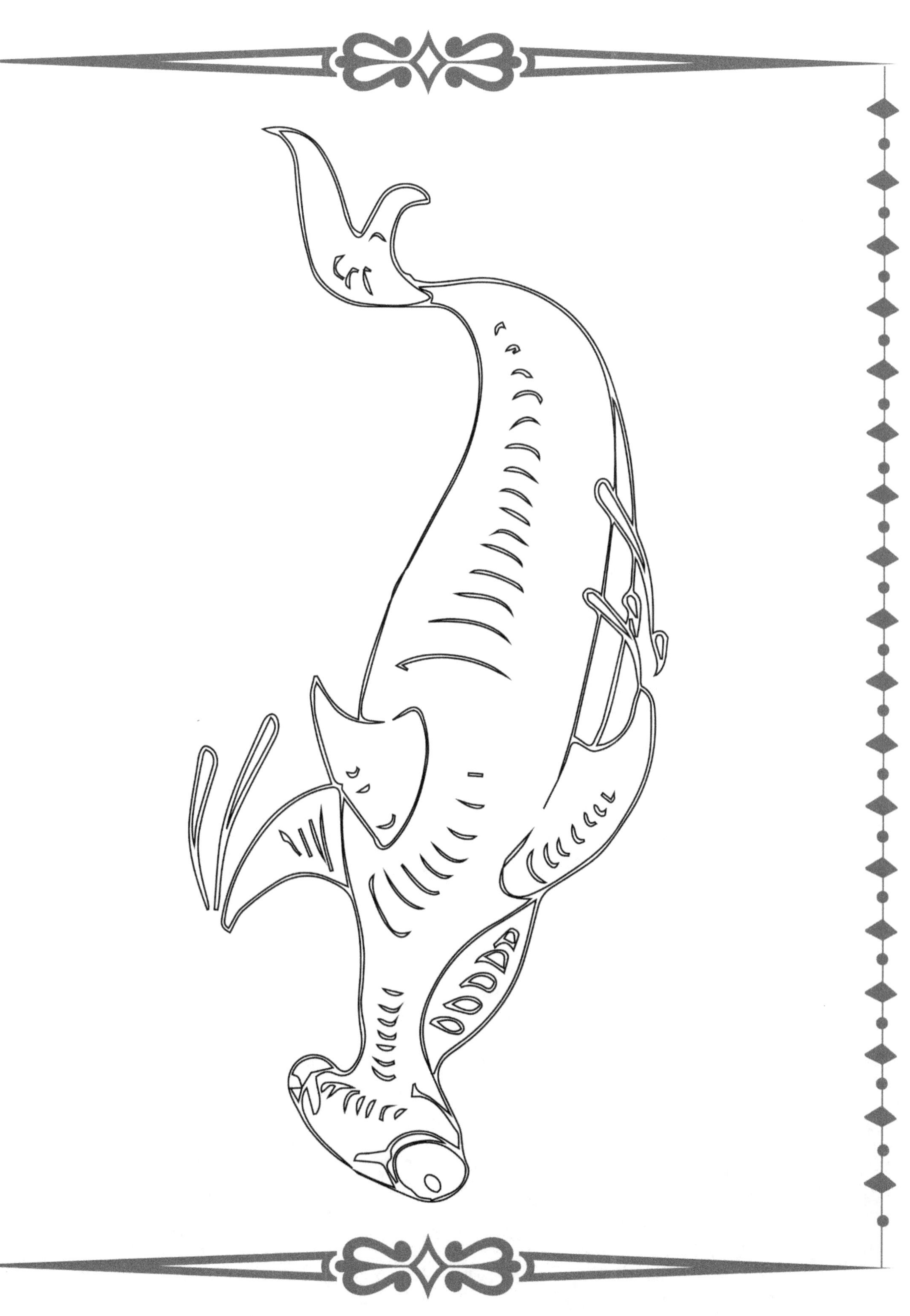

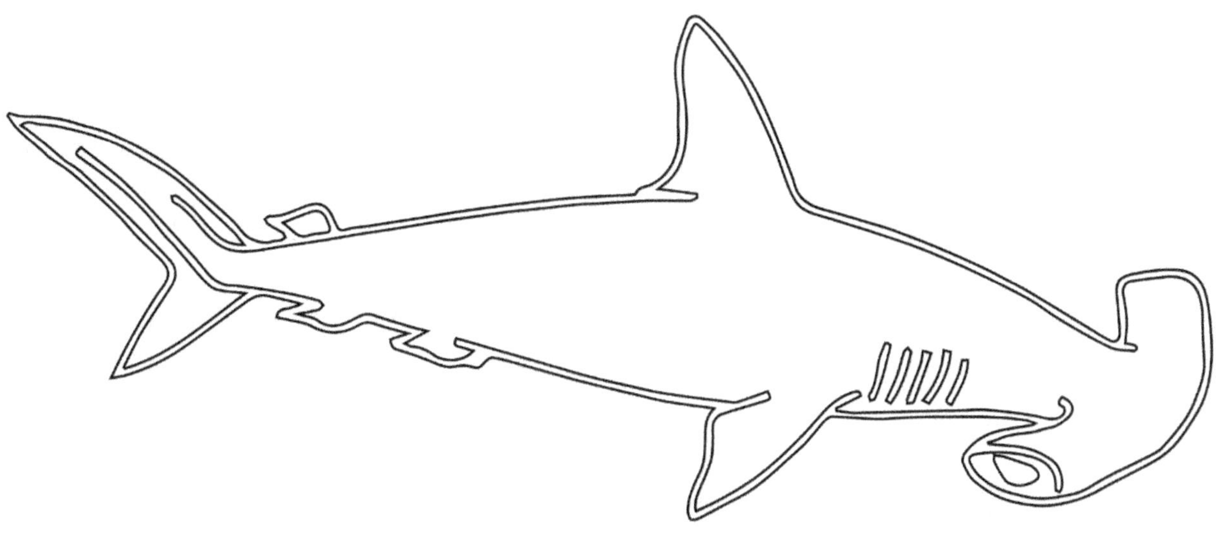

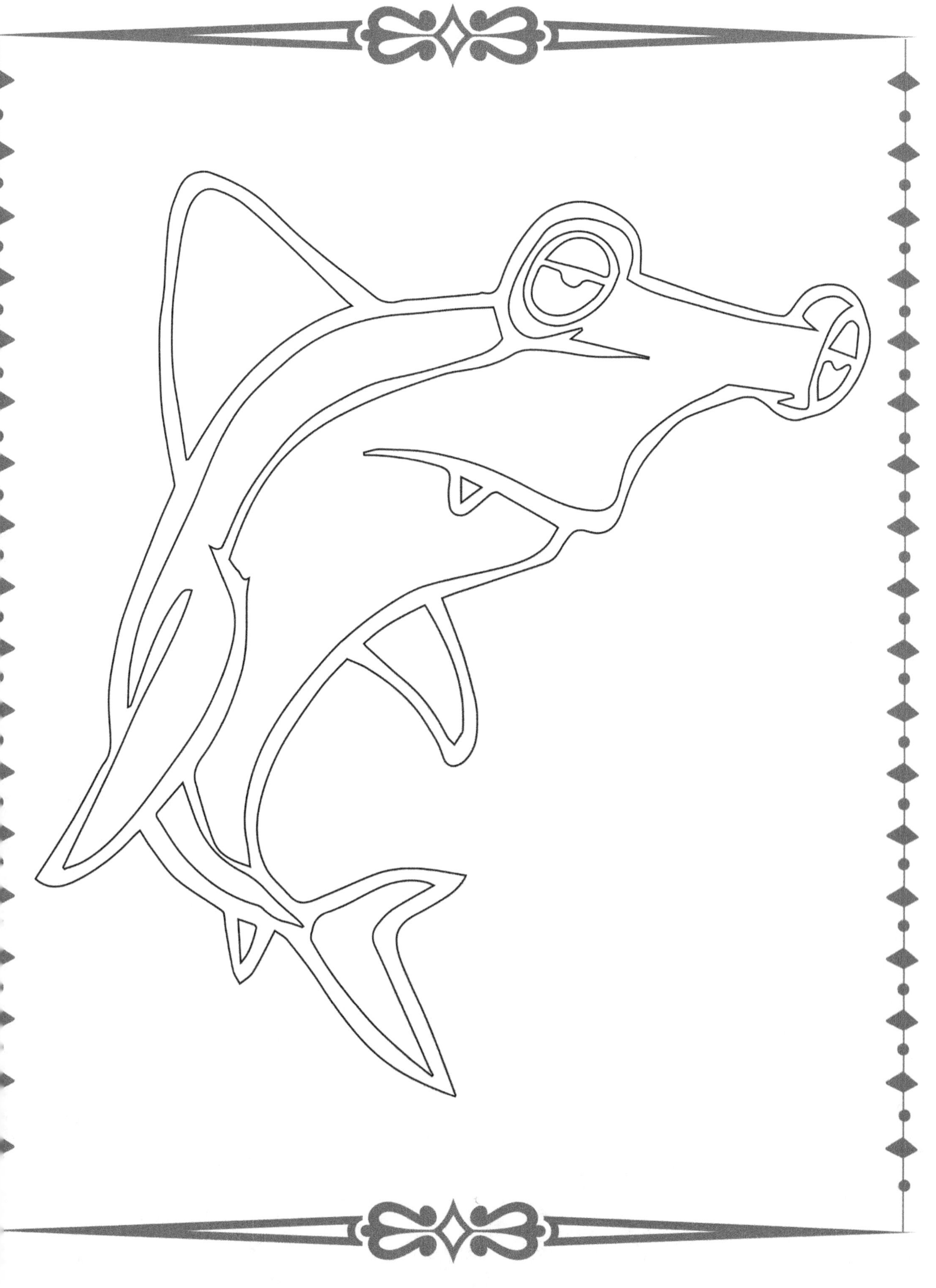

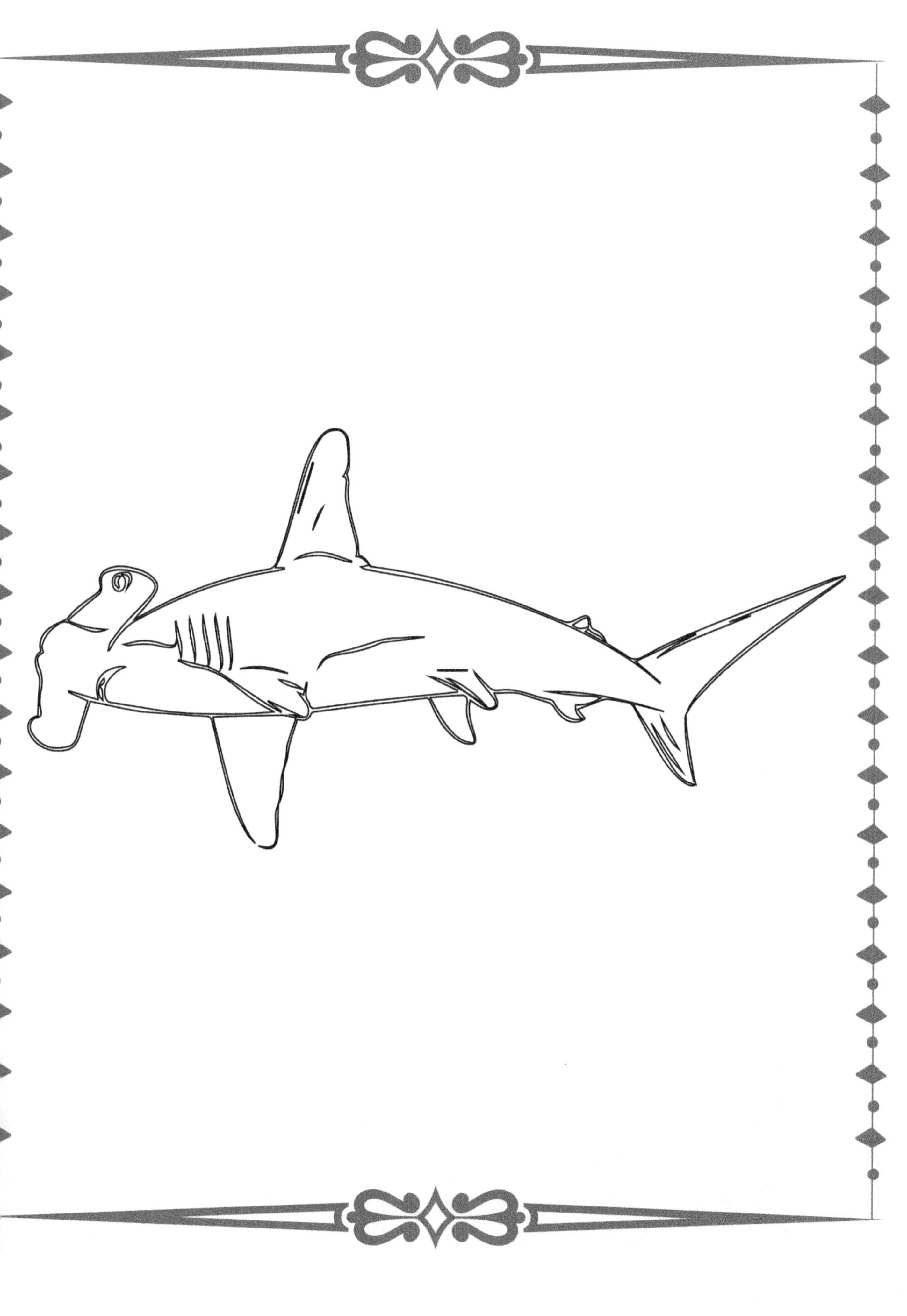

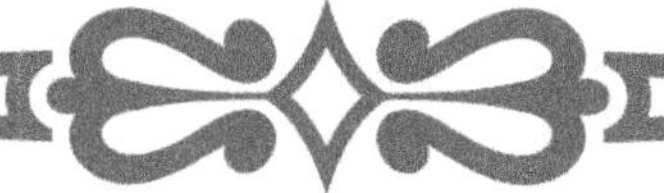

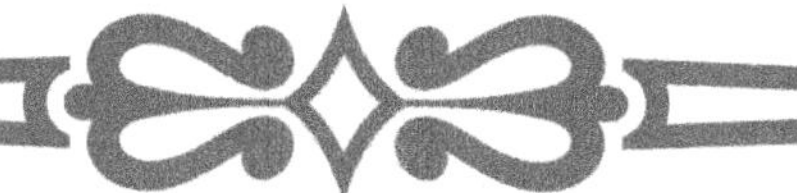

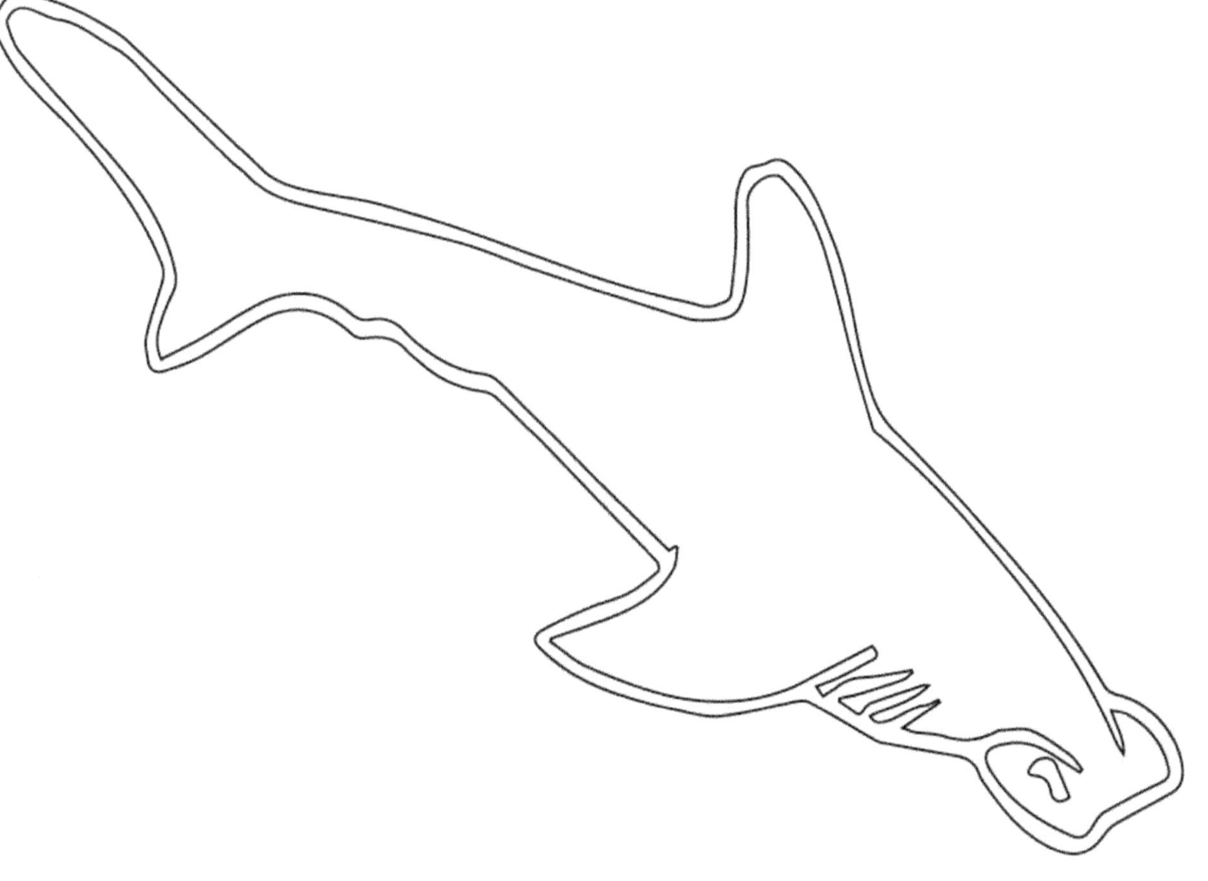

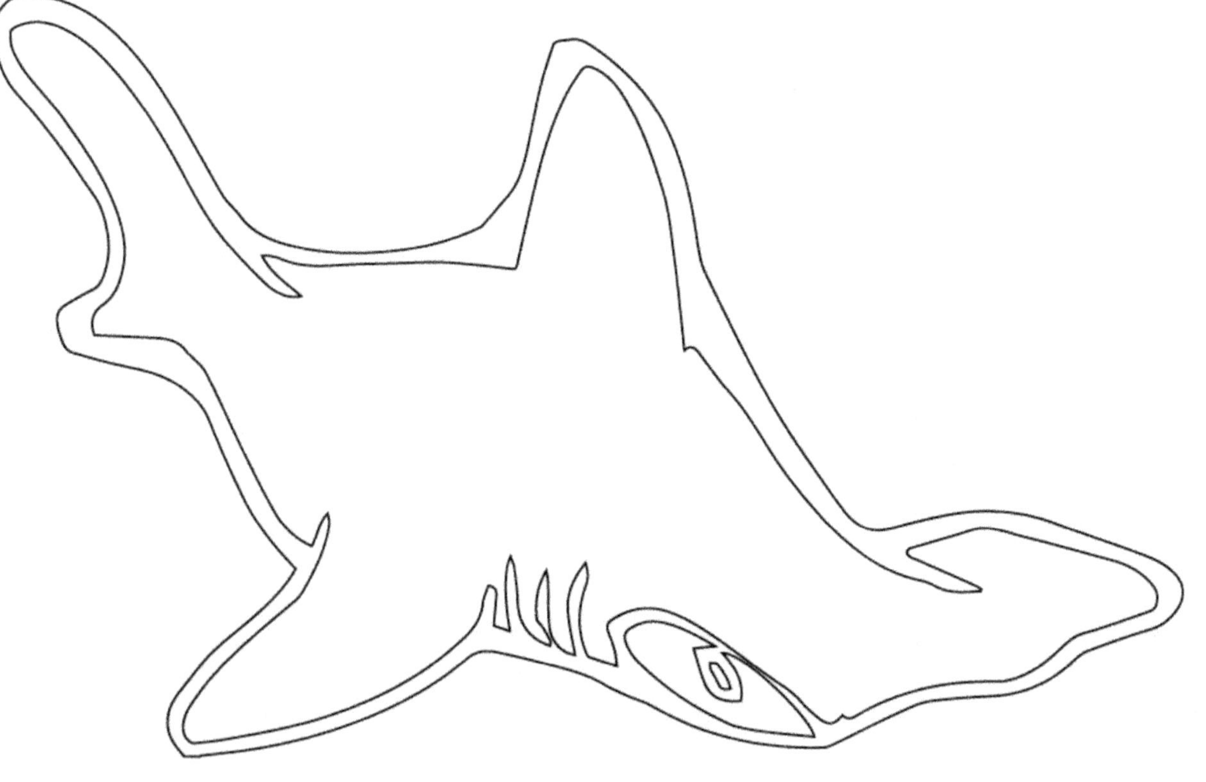